Danish Trivia Book

Interesting and Fun Facts
About Danish Culture, History,
Tourist Attractions, and Much
More

Alex Anderson

Contents

Chapter Three - Danish Geography   32

Chapter Four - Popular Danish Tourist Attraction Trivia 45

Danish Quiz to Test Yourself and Others 61

Conclusion 64

One last word from the author 65

References 66

Introduction

If you want to start talking about Denmark and the Danes, the first thing that comes to anyone's mind is happiness. Yes, happiness! Because Denmark has been adjudged the world's happiest country multiple times in the UN World Happiness Report. How can the Danes always find happiness? **Danes use simple ways to incorporate joy into their daily lives.**

The electrical sockets in Denmark have a smiley face. Seeing happy faces every time they pass by an electrical socket in their homes and offices reminds the Danes to smile and be happy. The smiley faces remind them to unplug from their busy schedules too.

Eating simple, delicious meals with family and friends is one of the easiest and best ways to be happy. Denmark has many communal eating spots where they meet with friends and family to eat and be happy. And the Danish pastry comes right on top of the most favorite Danish foods (more on this later).

Hygge is the Danish "thing" for happiness. It is a unique Danish word that represents the happiness that comes with spending quality time with friends and loved ones. Hygge could come in any form, including candle-lit dinners with your beloved, relaxed nights at home with your family, drinking wine with friends, and anything else that makes people happy.

Denmark reeks of elegant simplicity. The Danes love "simple," which is found everywhere, in their decor, design, lifestyle, etc. Simple almost always translates to happiness. Other government-aided reasons for Denmark's happiness include a 33-hour work week and a minimum wage of US$20. Even the US (believed to be one of the most developed nations in the world) has a minimum wage of US$10!

Health, good clean air, and happiness are inseparable triplets unique to Denmark. People in Denmark take their physical health very seriously, and for this, they have inculcated cycling as one of the most common forms of local transport. You can find people cruising happily on numerous scenic cycle routes in this bike-friendly country. Nine out of every ten Danes own a cycle, and many have more than one cycle.

If you are looking to throw around interesting facts about Denmark at a party or any other social gathering, you have come to the perfect place. The beautiful Scandinavian nation is replete with interesting facts and legendary tales that can hold the attention of any kind of audience in any social setting.

Moreover, your popularity among your friends and family will soar as you rattle off exciting and fun facts described in the form of unforgettable stories given in this book. So, turn the page and read more about Denmark, officially called the Kingdom of Denmark.

Chapter One - Danish Culture and Society

While unwelcome by many other countries, the high tax rates could be one reason for the Danish people's sense of happiness. Paying high taxes, perhaps, is a way for the Danes to reiterate the concept of hygge. Togetherness is the key element in Danish culture and society and covers everything, including money through taxes that the government uses to fund the country's free education, healthcare, and infrastructure needs for the entire country's benefit.

While on the topic of education, a unique feature in Denmark is that nearly 10% of all preschools are forest preschools. Located amidst woodlands, these schools help children connect with nature even as they learn modern subjects. In urban areas like Copenhagen, children can study in countryside environments. Like this, multiple other unique and special features define Danish culture and society.

No Danish Word for "Please"

It is not that Danes are impertinent or rude. It's just that their language does not have a direct translation or equivalent for the English word "please." And yet, the Danes are one of the politest people in the world. Foreigners traveling to Denmark are advised to use "tak," the Danish word for thank you, twice instead of "please." While on languages, an interesting fact about the Danes is that most of them are multilingual, enjoying learning at least one foreign language. The common languages spoken in Denmark are Danish, German, Norwegian, and English.

Hygge - Danish Cozy Togetherness

The word "hygge" (it is pronounced "hoo-ga") is not only unique to the Danish language but has become a global synonym for "cozy togetherness." Hygge relates to the feeling of happiness and well-being, an essence deeply ensconced in Danish culture and society.

Even the quaint, cobbled streets lined with vintage boutiques, little coffee shops, and beautifully designed colorful homes represent hygge as they invite you to take intimate walks through them. A classic way of Danish hygge is that if the weather turns bad, a Dane will not complain. They would simply curl up with a book and a hot cup of cocoa.

Hygge is the reason (or the cause) for the Danes' love for family and children. Mothers are entitled to up to 14 weeks of maternity leave with full pay, while fathers are entitled to two weeks of paternal leave with full pay. Further, when the child has reached 14 weeks, the parents get 32 weeks of leave (between them) to take care of the child's growing needs.

The Danish Pastry

Did you know that the world-famous Danish pastry is actually Austrian in origin? Austrian bakers who migrated to Denmark in the 1840s introduced these yummy pastries to the country, so the pastries are called "wienerbrod" or Viennese bread. What the Austrians brought was perfected in Denmark.

Smørrebrød - the Danish Open Sandwich

Smørrebrød is another contribution of Denmark to global food cuisine. Smorrebrod comes from the Danish word for bread and butter. When it started around the early 19th century, specifically created to feed hungry, hardworking agricultural workers, smørrebrød was a simple rye bread with butter and the previous night's leftovers. However, today, smørrebrødan has evolved into a culinary art form. Restaurants all over Denmark and the world serve lavish and artfully designed open sandwiches.

The Danes Love Cycling

The cycling culture of Denmark is so prevalent that there are 12,000km of cycling tracks all across the country. More than half of Copenhagers use cycles to commute to and from work. The Copenhageners collectively pedal more than 1 million km a day! The flat, even, and smooth cycling tracks are a pleasure to cycle on.

Only 4 out of 10 people in Denmark own a car. An added advantage for cyclists is that there are no mountains in Denmark. The culture of cycling is so deeply embedded in Danish culture that there is a Cycling Embassy in the government. Of course, that new cars are heavily taxed to discourage their purchase, and use adds to the growth of the Danish cycling culture.

Three Additional Alphabets

The Danish Language, derived from Indo-European languages, has three more alphabets than the 26 English ones, namely Æ, Ø, and Å, increasing its existing complexity thanks to difficult pronunciations and many silent letters. Å can be written as AA, Ø can be written as OE, and Æ can be written as AE.

Weirdly Interesting Danish Rituals

The Danes have many weirdly interesting (especially in the context of the modern world) customs and rituals. There is an annual carnival called "Fastelavn) in which a barrel containing a black cat is batted against. Fastelavn (which means "the evening before Lent") is celebrated across Denmark in late February or early March. On Midsummer's Eve (called Sankt Hans), witches are burned at the stake.

Of course, these rituals are only symbolic today, and neither real cats nor people are hurt. Pictures of black cats are stuck on barrels, and only dolls representing witches are burned. Both these festivals have moved away from the "dark rituals" of yore and have become fun-filled children's festivals.

On the matter of festivals, the Danes love Christmas and celebrate it right through December. Commercial and shopping areas, parks, and homes are all lit up throughout the month of Christmas. The first community lighting of a Christmas tree happened in 1914 at Copenhagen's town square.

World's Oldest Amusement Parks in Denmark

The world's two oldest amusement parks are found in Denmark. The oldest one is Bakken (very close to Copenhagen), and the second oldest is Tivoli Gardens, which is right at the center of the capital, close to the city's train station. These old parks are a testament to the fact that the

Danes always sought happiness and joy and preferred being together and having fun over other things.

Bakken's legendary story goes like this. A lady called Kirsten Piil found a natural spring in a forest near Copenhagen. Copenhagen itself had very poor water conditions. So, the locals headed to this forest area for their water needs. They would take a day trip to this place to drink water!

Lego's Original Home Is in Denmark

The Lego company was established by a Danish carpenter named Ole Kirk Christiansen in 1932. The word "lego" comes from "leg godt," which translates to "play well." The Danish people really know how to play well. Another reason for their happiness, perhaps!

Ole Christiansen was making wooden toys, and the Lego Company he set up continued to make them until 1947 when they introduced the iconic interlocking plastic bricks that are now world-famous.

The original Legoland is a famous tourist destination (more of this is in the chapter on tourist spots in Denmark). Interestingly, since 2018, the plastic for the Lego bricks has been made from recycled sugarcane, enhancing the toy's eco-friendly status.

Denmark - the First to Legalized Same-Sex Marriages

One of the most forward-thinking nations in the world, Denmark was the first country to legalize same-sex marriages way back in 1989. Pride celebrations happen all over the country at frequent intervals.

Janteloven - the Danish Equality

An unwritten Danish law is this, "No one is better than another." Everyone in Danish society is accepted and embraced for what they are. All are equal and given the same respect and dignity due to any human being, regardless of their achievements. This "equal" mentality works very well for the entire nation of Denmark and is not relegated to only the seeming "achievers." The reason for the development of the Janteloven concept is to prevent people from becoming arrogant, vain, and thinking they are better than others.

Community Dinners

Places like Absalons Kirke reflect the laid-back, happy attitude of the Danish people who don't hesitate to find hygge every day. Absalons Kirke is an old church converted into a social gathering place where citizens and visitors can sit together, eat together (budget-friendly meals are also available), play games, and have a relaxed evening. It is a classic representation of Danish hygge. Places like Absalons Kirke make it difficult to leave Copenhagen without a happy smile on your face. Interestingly, the Danes love fine dining too, which is perhaps why Denmark has the highest number of Michelin-star restaurants in Europe.

Singletons and Spices

Unmarried men and women get cinnamon powder poured on them on their 25th birthdays. This tradition dates back hundreds of years when spice salesmen remained unmarried because they traveled a lot. It continues to be followed even today in Denmark. If you are unmarried on your 25th birthday, your friends and family will pour cinnamon powder over you so much that you will be covered in it. Sometimes, they will splash water over the person to make the powder stick.

In the olden days, spice salesmen rarely found a partner and were called Pebersvends (or pepper dudes), and a single woman was Pebermø (pepper maiden). The spice connection continues for those who remained unmarried until 30 because, on their 30th birthday, cinnamon gets replaced with pepper. Importantly, there is no judgment in these rituals because the average marriage age of Danish men is 34, and Danish women are 32. The use of cinnamon and pepper powders is not considered punishment, only pranks for fun.

Famous Modern Danes

Many Danes are world-famous, including actors like Brigitte Nielsen (Rocky and Red Sonya), Mads Mikkelsen (Hannibal, Casino Royale), Nikolaj Coster Waldau (Game of Thrones), and more. Famous sports stars from Denmark include Manchester United footballer Peter Schmeichel, tennis star Caroline Wozniacki, former professional boxer Mikkel Kessler, etc. Famous musicians from Denmark are Lukas Graham, Lars Ulrich, and MØ MØ.

Denmark Is a Country of Pioneers and Inventors

Denmark is not only a pioneer in toy making. Many Danes are pioneers and inventors in various fields. Here are a few of them:

- **Rasmus Malling Hansen** - In 1865, this Danish inventor designed the first commercially produced typewriter, the Hansen Writing Ball. He was the principal of the Royal Institute for the Deaf.

- **Frederik Louis Wilhelm** Hellesen - In 1887, this Danish industrialist and inventor designed the first dry-cell battery. He sold the first batteries to the Danish Telephone Company in 1889.

- **Valdemar Poulsen** - In 1899, this Danish engineer invented the telegraphone, the earliest magnetic sound recording device.

- **Jens and Lars Rasmussen** - These two brothers founded a mapping-related startup, the precursor to present-day Google Maps.

- **Sydney's landmark**, the Royal Opera House, was designed by a Dane.

Ten Interesting Facts about Danish Culture and Society

1. Children are not entirely restricted from drinking. Drinks can be sold to children depending on their age and the alcoholic content.

2. The government controls the naming of children. There is a government-approved list of around 7000 names that parents can choose from, and they cannot use a name outside of this list. Even odd spelling of approved names cannot be used.

3. Burning Danish flags anywhere in the country is perfectly legal. However, burning any other country's flag is illegal.

4. The world's cleanest tap water is found in Denmark. There is no need for you to buy bottled water here. You can drink straight from the tap. The water in Copenhagen's harbor (mostly dirty and unhygienic in many countries) is clean enough to swim, and people often swim there.

5. Jaywalking is taken very seriously in Denmark, with hefty fines of up to 1000 DKK (approx. 130 Euros!) Therefore, in Denmark, do not cross the road anywhere but the pedestrian crossing, and only after the traffic lights say "GO!" This rule should be strictly followed even when the roads are clear.

6. The elderly assistance program in Denmark allows people over 65 to retire with a comfortable pension. Those above 60 can also invoke something called "redundancy," wherein they can stop working and still get a percentage of their salary until they are 65 when they become eligible for a pension. Also, when the elderly cannot live alone even with

government-funded assistance, they are shifted to elderly care facilities.

7. The average Dane is known to drink four cups of coffee per day. The Danes love to eat salty licorice with a glass of cold milk.

8. The Danish people prefer to see dentists in Poland and Hungary, thanks to the prohibitively expensive costs in Denmark.

9. There is a TV channel in Denmark for kids alone. With no commercial breaks, the characters of this channel go to sleep when it is bedtime for kids.

10. The world's largest manufacturer of wind turbines is a Danish company called Vestas, another reason for the country's green credentials. About 40% of the country's electricity needs are met through wind power.

Chapter Two - Danish History

The areas comprising present-day Denmark are believed to have been inhabited since 12500 BCE. Archeological findings from this area date back to 130,000 to 110,000 BCE. Agricultural pieces of evidence can be dated back to about 3900 BCE. Experts opine that since the last Ice Age (around 10,000 BCE), people from Southern and Eastern Europe migrated to northern regions, modern-day Denmark, thanks to the country's rich, flat, and fertile plains and proximity to water.

Interestingly, the harsh climate also shaped this country's history, culture, and society. Between the 9th and 11th centuries, Viking warriors from the Scandinavian region, including Denmark, raided much of Europe. The modern cities of Denmark were established after the Viking Age.

The Earliest Danes

The earliest humans in Denmark were hunter-gatherers and fishermen believed to have migrated from other parts of Europe around 10,000 BCE. Farming started around 3,000 BCE, thanks to the abundance of flat land and fertile soil. They used stone to make their tools and weapons (during the

Stone Age) and moved to use bronze and iron (during the Bronze and Iron Ages).

The Danes have had trade links with the Roman Empire from the Iron Age, trading in amber, animal furs, etc. The Rune language is believed to have evolved by 200 ACE.

The Vikings of Denmark

Known to be one of the most notorious periods in Danish history, the Viking Ages started around 793 ACE, wherein the Vikings from Denmark first raided Lindisfarne, an English island. These violent raids continued for 250 years, during which time the Vikings controlled parts of Northern England and Northwestern France.

At one time in Viking history, their rule extended way beyond Denmark and included parts of Norway, Sweden, the Faroe Islands, Greenland, Orkney, and Shetland, along with parts of England, France, and Germany. York was the English capital of Vikings.

The Vikings were excellent navigators and seamen. They traveled far and wide, even to present-day Turkey, Russia, and North America. Interestingly, they plundered, looted, and stole their way through the places they landed and indulged in peaceful trades in metals, glassware, textiles, fur, jewelry, and even enslaved Europeans.

An interesting fact about Vikings is this. Shakespeare's Hamlet is based on an ancient Viking prince, Amled of Jutland.

The Danish Monarchy Is the Oldest in Europe

The Danish monarchy dates back to 935 ACE. The current monarchy was established by Gorm the Old (who ruled Denmark from circa 936 until his death in 958) and continues to hold sway over Denmark today. Gorm the Old raised a runestone for his wife, Queen Thyra. In ancient times, usually, the eldest son of the reigning monarch or the closest male relative would succeed to the throne, and by this Gorm, the Old was succeeded by his son King Harald Bluetooth.

Christianity in Denmark

King Harald Bluetooth was baptized in 965 ACE, after which Christianity spread rapidly throughout the kingdom, although neighboring kingdoms to the south of Denmark had already converted to Christianity. Archbishop Willbrod, who traveled from England, was the first Christian missionary to Denmark.

The then Danish King Ongendus was unwelcoming, so the archbishop, describing the Danish king as "crueler than any animal and harder than stone," returned to England. Also, the Vikings learned a lot about Christianity during their travels and were impressed with the mighty churches and cathedrals found in the Christian kingdoms they traveled to.

So, when King Harald Bluetooth was baptized in 965 ACE, Christian clergy became very influential and powerful in Denmark, and its spread happened quickly after that.

The Kalmar Union and Denmark

In the late 14th century, Queen Margrethe I unified Sweden, Denmark (which included Iceland and Greenland), and Norway under the Kalmar Union. Sweden left the union in 1523, but Denmark continued to rule over Norway for many years until 1814.

After the breakup, Denmark and Sweden fought each other regularly for control of various territories until 1658, when Denmark had to concede Skåne, Halland, and Blekinge, the present-day southern provinces of Sweden.

After losing these three provinces to Sweden, Denmark introduced absolute and hereditary monarchy, which resulted in the creation of a well-organized bureautic state, thanks to the absence of revolts and power-grabbing tactics among the other Danish nobles. Consequently, efficient reforms, especially in the field of agriculture, came to be implemented, leading to the kingdom's growth and development.

The Constitution of Denmark

The Danish Constitution was first signed on June 5th, 1849, after decades of absolute monarchy. It was signed by King Frederick VII, who declared Denmark a constitutional monarchy, a system of government wherein the monarch's power is limited to a prescribed legal framework. Denmark's' constitution has been revised four times since then, including one in 1915 when women were given the right to vote. The last amendment was done in 1953. June 5th is celebrated as Constitution Day speeches by politicians, flag hoisting, church congregations, and more.

Denmark and Germany Wars

A power struggle always existed between the German Confederation and the Danish Kings over the control of Schleswig, Holstein, and Lauenburg, duchies located in the Jutland Peninsula on Denmark's south border with Germany. The First and Second Schleswig Wars were fought between Germany and Denmark to control these territories.

The Danes won the First Schleswig (also called Dane-Prussia) War fought between 1848 and 1851. However, tensions between the two nations continued resulting in the Second Schleswig War in 1864. The Kingdom of Denmark had to cede the three duchies to the Germans this time around. However, in 1920, the northern parts of these territories, which were predominantly Danish, were given back to Denmark, thanks to the results of a plebiscite, ably aided by Germany's defeat in World War I.

Mass Emigration to the US

The forty years between 1880 and 1920 saw some unprecedented migration numbers in Denmark. Nearly 10% of Denmark's population migrated to the US during this time. These early immigrants had little choice but to find greener pastures outside of Denmark, which was hit by an unprecedented increase in population. There were not enough jobs in the country, forcing some people to leave. Further, after Schleswig was ceded to Germany, Danish culture underwent a period of repression, adding to the immigration.

World War I and Denmark

When WWI broke out, Denmark declared its neutrality. Many neutral countries were involved in supplying food to the nations that were at war. Food exports contributed significantly to the country's revenue, and to run this business in and for countries on both sides of the war called for immense diplomatic and political discretion.

Danish housewives were motivated to learn how to prepare nutritious and delicious food during those trying times when supplies of raw materials dwindled. This major Danish endeavor was called the "Battle for Food 1914 - 1918." This battle did not have a singularly military outlook but extended to the nutrition of both warring and neutral countries.

This food crisis endeavor continues to motivate Denmark and its people to fight against food waste, an important cultural aspect discussed in Chapter 1.

Denmark after World War I

The Battle for Food put Denmark ahead in the food production industry. Farmers cooperative movements aided the Danish economy in leaps and bounds. There was a paradigm shift from cultivation to livestock farming and dairy production, industries founded on the advantages of industrialization. After World War I, Denmark established an efficient social welfare state.

World War II and Denmark

During World War II, Denmark and Germany agreed they would not attack each other. But Germany broke the promise and attacked Denmark in 1940, after which it ruled over the Danish people, although the country was allowed to keep its own government. The Danes developed an underground resistance movement against Nazi rule throughout the five-year German rule. Finally, with the help of the Grand Alliance, comprising the US, the UK, and the Soviet Union, the Nazis were defeated, and Denmark was free on May 5th, 1945.

Denmark after World War II

The Danish economy after World War II improved even more, with increasing exports contributing significantly to the country's economic growth. Various goods from Denmark, including furniture, Danish designs, butter, and bacon, became exceedingly popular all over the world. Denmark was one of the founding members of the United Nations. The country joined the Economic European Community (EEC, which later became the European Union) in 1972.

Today, Denmark stands for the defense of human rights, free trade, and liberal society. The country is known to help in the fight against world poverty. The liberal attitude is reflected in the country being the first to introduce women into its parliament in 1918 (even before the US gave its women the right of suffrage) and, of course, being the first nation to legalize same-sex marriages.

The Danes Love the Royal Family

According to a Gallup survey conducted in 2014, 82% of the Danish people did not favor abolishing the monarchy and believed Denmark benefited greatly from the royal family. The current head of the royal family is Queen Margrethe II, only the second woman to ascend the Danish throne after Queen Margrethe I, who died in 1412.

The Danish royals love their people with equal vigor, and this two-way love and respect is why the Danish monarchy stays relevant even today. The down-to-earth behavior of the Danish royals inspires feelings of equality in Danish society. The Danish monarchy is royal yet grounded and humble. It is common for royals to be seen cycling through the streets, doing gardening, and dropping their children at school like everyone else. Importantly, the modern Danish royals are known to marry for love, and not just any other royal.

An Interesting Ongoing Land Dispute between Denmark and Canada

A small 1.3 square km island in the middle of Nares Strait is a bone of contention between Denmark and Canada, as both claim it as theirs. This little island is within the 12-km territorial limit of both nations and, therefore, the dispute over it. Interestingly, there is no rancor between the nations in this conflict. It is a peaceful disagreement. Every month, representatives from Denmark and Canada come to this island, plant their respective flags, and leave behind a bottle of their favorite liquor. The Danes leave Danish schnapps, and the Canadians leave Canadian whiskey.

The Oldest University in Denmark

The University of Copenhagen was established way back on June 1, 1479, by King Christian I. It is one of the oldest universities in Northern Europe and is Denmark's biggest educational and research institution. When founded, it had four branches of study: Law, Medicine, Theology, and Philosophy. Today, the University of Copenhagen is one of Northern Europe's largest Health and Life Sciences places of learning and research.

Ten Interesting Facts about Danish History

1. Constitution Day is not an official public holiday. But shops and businesses are closed after mid-day.

2. Denmark is a member of NATO, EEC, EU, and UN.

3. Bluetooth is named after King Harald Bluetooth, the eldest son of Gorm, the Old, and the monarch who unified Denmark into a single kingdom. The iconic symbol of Bluetooth is a combination of the runic alphabets for 'H" and "B."

4. The oldest operating film company in the world is Nordisk Film. It has been in existence in Copenhagen since 1906.

5. Denmark is part of the EU, but Euro is not its currency. It is the Danish Kroner.

6. The Great Dane that the Danish people claim is their breed of dog is actually from Germany.

7. One of the Danish princes is a catwalk model. The young Prince Nikolai, the ninth in line to the Danish throne, debuted in 2018 at the London Fashion Week for Burberry. He continues to

model for other large, niche brands like Dior.

8. The fame of the Danes is not restricted to the Vikings. The best-known fairy tale writer, Hans Christian Andersen, was a Dane.

9. Nearly 99% of the Jewish population in Denmark survived the Nazi Holocaust because the Danes helped evacuate all of them to Sweden, a neutral country not under the control of the Nazis.

10. The first Gothic brick cathedral is Roskilde Cathedral in Danish Zealand. From here on, the architectural trend to use bricks to build churches and cathedrals began.

Chapter Three - Danish Geography

Often, the Scandinavian area is visualized as a vast expanse of land filled with fjords, mountains, and lakes. However, in reality, Denmark is a small country, and in terms of size falls somewhere between West Virginia and Maryland in the US. The country of Denmark is made up of the Jutland Peninsula and more than 440 islands, with less than 80 of them being inhabited.

Denmark is nestled between the Baltic Sea and the North Sea. Denmark has a constitutional monarchy form of government, and its capital city is Copenhagen. Copenhagen was founded 800 years ago but became the capital city in 1443.

Located in northern Europe, Denmark's southern border with Germany is about 68 km in length. The melting of the glaciers and their gradual movement towards land mass during the Ice Age shaped the country as it is today, mostly flat plains with gently rolling hills and a long coastline replete with inlets, gulfs, and lagoons. The warm waters of the Gulf Stream cut through the biting cold, making Denmark warmer than the other parts of Northern Europe.

Here are some interesting and fun facts about the geography of this Scandinavian country.

The World's Oldest Flag

The Danish flag, called "Dannebrog," was first acknowledged in 1219, making it the oldest continuously used official flag of any independent country in the world. The white cross on a red background is one of the most recognizable flags in the world. Legend tells us that this flag fell from the sky (yes, sent by the gods living up there) in Estonia in 1219 during the Battle of Lyndanisse. This inspired the Danes to victory against the Latvians. About a century later, the Danish rulers adopted this gift from their gods as their flag.

No Mountains in Denmark

One of the primary reasons biking became popular in Denmark is the utter lack of mountains and mountainous terrains. The highest natural point in Denmark, called Møllehøj, is just 170 m above sea level. This peak is located in the eastern part of the country.

Greenland Belongs to Denmark

The humongous ice territory of Greenland belongs to the Kingdom of Denmark. However, it is considered an autonomous constituent country with Denmark having some control over it and, therefore, is not included as Denmark's territory for the sake of size and population. So, Denmark is both a small and a huge country!

Greenland is bound entirely by the Arctic Ocean and the North Atlantic Ocean so it has an arctic climate. Snow never melts on this island of ice. In fact, with every new snowfall, layers of ice get compressed, and in some places, the height of fallen snow is over 1,500 m (nearly 10 times higher than the highest natural peak of Denmark, Møllehøj).

Five Regions of Denmark

Denmark is divided into five regions. These were established under the aegis of the 2007 Danish Municipal Reform, wherein the earlier traditional counties were abolished, and these five regions were created. This reform was designed to radically reduce the power of regional governments while simultaneously increasing the power of local and central governments in Copenhagen. Let us look at each of these regions in a bit of detail.

1. Region Hovedstaden

2. Region Midtjylland

3. Region Nordjylland

4. Region Sjælland

5. Region Syddanmark

Region Hovedstaden

Also referred to as the "Capital Region of Denmark," this region lies in northern Denmark. It is connected to Sweden through the Oresund Bridge. Lake Arresø, Denmark's largest lake, is located here. Moreover, the rising of this area because of the post-glacial rebound has created multiple lakes from former bays and inlets.

Region Midtjylland

The Central Denmark Region, or Midtjylland, is often called Mid Jutland. It borders Limfjord in the northwest, the North Sea in the west, and Kattegat in the east. The Central Denmark Region includes the islands of Samsø, Anholt, Endelave, Tunø, Hjarnø, Alrø, Venø, Jegindø, and Fur. Inland heaths and coastal dunes characterize the western parts of this region, while the eastern, slightly hilly areas are dotted with forests, streams, and lakes, making the land in this region very fertile.

Region Nordjylland

This region is also referred to as the North Jutland Region or North Denmark Region. One of the five universities in Denmark, Aalborg University, is located in Region Nordjylland. John F. Kennedy

Square, named in honor of the 35th President of the United States, is a famous landmark in Aalborg and reiterates the Danish-US friendship. You can also visit the Aalborg Zoo, established in 1935, here.

Region Sjælland

Region Sjælland, or Region Zealand, is the southernmost region in Denmark. The capital city of Region Sjælland is Sorø. According to legend, Gefjun, the Norse Goddess of agriculture, abundance, and fertility, created Denmark. One day, she approached King Gylfi of Sweden, disguised as a poor, homeless woman seeking help from the generous king.

The king told her that she could have as much land as four oxen could plow in one day. Goddess Gefjun thanked the king and called her four sons, born of a powerful giant. She transformed them into oxen. They not only plowed a large section of the land but also broke it away from Sweden, resulting in Lake Malaren's formation. This land that was torn away from Sweden by the goddess' son came to be known as Zealand.

Region Syddanmark

Region Syddanmark, or the Region of Southern Denmark, forms the westernmost part of Denmark. The capital city of this region is Vejle.

There are many mountain peaks in this region (more than 500 unnamed ones), all of which are less than 170 m tall. As mentioned earlier, Denmark is a flat land with the highest natural peak, Møllehøj being only 170m in height.

Faroe Islands

The Faroe Islands are part of the Kingdom of Denmark geographically. But it is self-governing. Located between Norway and Denmark, the Faroe Islands is a group of 18 volcanic islands with a population of just over 50,000. The original inhabitants of the Faroe Islands, the Faroese, are descendants of Norwegian settlers who came to Denmark from Norway.

The Climate of Denmark

Being in the North Temperate Zone, the average temperature in summer is about 16 degrees C. Short spurts of snowfall are experienced from December until March. Rain is also common during this time. Between January and February, the temperature remains just about 0 degrees C.

The activities of the Danish people are aligned with the seasons. During the winters, the Danes are focused on enjoying "hygge," relaxing with friends and family over delicious food and drink. The Danes indulge in outdoor activities during the summer, including cycling, sailing, and hiking.

Denmark's Coastline and Beaches

Denmark's coastline is over 7,300 km long and is perfect for beaches, harbors, and fishing spots. In fact, thanks to the beautiful coastline, Denmark's tourism's solid foundation is on the strength of these three industries. Denmark is home to more than 170 Blue Flag beaches and 15 Blue Flag marinas. Some of the top beach holiday destinations of the world are in Denmark, including but certainly not limited to:

- Søndervig Beach in West Jutland

- Blåvand Beach in West Jutland

- Blokhus Beach

- Rømø Beach

Lakes of Denmark

Denmark has thousands of named and unnamed lakes across its mainland and numerous islands. Two of the largest and most beautiful lakes in the country are:

Arresø - It is the largest lake in Denmark, covering an area of over 39 square km. It is located in the north of Island Zealand, draining into Roskilde Fjord via the Arresø Canal. Before it became a lake, Arresø was a fjord. But tectonic activities in the area turned it into a lake by cutting it from the sea. The lake is a beautiful abode of diverse flora and birds. It comes under the jurisdiction of the Kongernes Nordsjælland National Park.

Esrum - The second largest lake in Denmark is Esrum covering an area of over 17 square km. This lake is situated in the central part of North Zealand, bordering Gribskov, the country's largest forest area. The royal family's official home is on the banks of this beautiful lake. A variety of birds, including common goldeneye, tufted duck, mute swan, etc., and fish such as the European perch, northern pike, etc., make their home in and around Lake Esrum.

Stadil Fjord - Despite its name, Stadil Fjord is a freshwater lake and not a fjord. It is known for its splendid natural beauty, characterized by meadows, reed forests, and farmlands along its banks. It is a very clean lake and is a popular spot for cyclists and hikers.

Other large lakes in the country include Mossø (on the eastern side of Jutland), Saltbæk Vig (a brackish lake in West Zealand), and Lake Furesø (the deepest lake in Denmark with a maximum depth of over 37 m).

Denmark Celebrates the Fourth of July

Yes, the friendship between Denmark and the US is evident because the Danes celebrate the Fourth of July with as much gusto as the Americans. This tradition goes back to the mass migration period in the 1800s when many Danes migrated to the Americas in search of better opportunities.

The Danish-American Society of Chicago purchased a hilly terrain in Jutland and planted the entire area with the traditional heather, a flowering plant that made this area beautiful. The society then gifted the land to King Christian IX on the condition that the beauty of this area should be retained as it is and that the American Independence should be officially celebrated every year in this place.

Since then, the Fourth of July has been a kind of homecoming for Danish Americans. In fact, returning home to Denmark for this celebration is still seen as a pilgrimage for many Danish Americans, showing their love and respect for both their home countries.

Plants and Animals Native to Denmark

Denmark is home to many native trees and plants. The forests of Denmark are dotted with pines, spruces, and other conifer trees. Deciduous trees such as maples, oaks, sycamores, and more can also be found. The country used to have forests filled with Scots pine which had all disappeared. Now, the Scots pine is being reintroduced everywhere in the country, and they are thriving again.

The national flower of Denmark is the red clover. This flower has been used medicinally for thousands of years thanks to the presence of estrogen-like compounds. Other common plants found in Denmark include:

- **Swiss cheese plant** - The name comes from the fact that the leaves of this popular house plant have holes in them.

- **Red fescue** - This perennial grass is used for erosion control all over Denmark. It can be manicured and, therefore, used in landscapes too.

- **Creeping bent** - Another common perennial grass used for landscaping and in gardens, and commonly used in golf turfs.

Animals native to Denmark include:

- Orca (one of the largest killer whales in the world)

- Beluga whale (also called melonhead)

- Red deer (you can find them all over Europe)

- Wild boar (also called the Eurasian wild pig)

- Harp seal (also called saddleback and Greenland seal)

- Walrus

- Raccoon

- Gray wolf

- Siberian chipmunk

Also, thanks to the long coastline filled with gulfs, inlets, and fjords, over 300 species of birds inhabit Denmark. The country's coastline is an ideal habitat for all kinds of waterfowl, the most common ones being swans, herons, and storks.

Ten Interesting Facts about Danish Geography

1. You are always close to the sea while in Denmark. The furthest distance from the sea anywhere in the country is 52 km.

2. It rains in Denmark for nearly 170 days every year.

3. Denmark is an actively agricultural country producing three times its food needs. Therefore, it is a major exporter of agricultural and dairy products.

Denmark's butter and hams are popular all across Europe.

4. Denmark is proud to be known as the "least corrupt nation" in the entire world.

5. Freetown is a "state within a state," a neighborhood created by the hippies of Denmark in 1971. Freetown is also called "The Green Light District," and certain liberties with regard to the sale and use of drugs are allowed here, although it is illegal in Denmark. Freetown represents an alternative lifestyle option for those who want.

6. The Danes are very conscious and aware of their beautiful environment. There are strict pollution-related laws in place to maintain nature's beauty. Further, Copenhagen has a plan in place to make the capital city carbon neutral by 2025.

7. Denmark is one of the top fishing countries in the world. However, it is going through an aquaculture crisis currently. There are limits on fishing specific species of fish. Still, Denmark continues to rank among the top fishing nations in the world. Eighteen different

species of sharks are known to inhabit Danish waters.

8. Denmark is home to five major universities, including its oldest one (the University of Copenhagen), which opened in 1479. The other five universities are Aarhus University, Technical University of Denmark, Aalborg University, and Copenhagen Business School.

9. Religion is not a big driving force in Denmark. Yet, social and family events like baptisms, weddings, funerals, etc., are taken seriously and done religiously. Women are accepted into the clergy in Denmark.

10. Thanks to the high latitude, summers in Denmark have long days, sometimes extending to more than 17 hours. During this time, the sky hardly ever gets dark.

Chapter Four - Popular Danish Tourist Attraction Trivia

One of the first things you learned about Denmark is it is small. But that does not make the country any less beautiful. In fact, being small is what makes it beautiful and easy to explore, especially for tourists. Yes, despite the absence of mountains, or rather, because of the absence of mountains.

As a tourist, there are different modes of transport available to you. Public transport is easily accessible and inexpensive.

- You can cycle with the locals and use electric scooters

- You can take the well-connected Harbor Bus and long-distance coach travel system.

- The 24/7 metro system in Copenhagen is at your service.

- You can utilize the easy-to-access railway system across the country.

- Ferries are available to the many picturesque islands of the country.

- Daily flights are also available from Copenhagen to other cities in Denmark.

Get ready to go knee-deep into hygge during winters and do the outdoors as the adventurous Danes do during summers. Denmark is all about fun and having a good time because that's what the Danes believe too. They happily extend their hospitality to visitors and beckon everyone with open arms to explore their stunning cities and villages.

Bakken and Tivoli Gardens

Bakken was established in 1583 when a natural spring was discovered in the area. The people of Copenhagen flocked to this place because the water quality in their living areas was poor. As more people came to the spring to spend their leisure time, entertainers and hawkers followed to serve the crowds.

Today, Bakken, officially called Dyrehavsbakken, is located in the woods of Dyrehaven, very close to Copenhagen, and is filled with thrill rides, amusement games, and a variety of food stalls. It has a lot to offer for both adults and children. It is a perfect place of leisure for the whole family. Considering its antiquity, it would be a shame if you came to Denmark and did not visit Bakken, an amusement park filled with history and nostalgia. Entry is free!

Compared to Bakken, Tivoli Gardens is relatively new. It opened in 1843, almost 250 years after Bakken. Located at the center of Copenhagen, Tivoli Gardens is a world-class amusement park that inspired Walt Disney to dream about building a "great, great playground for children."

In addition to some great rides and games, Tivoli Gardens offers a range of live concerts and light shows. You can pick up your favorite food from any of the multiple restaurants and food places there and have a picnic in the gardens. Tivoli Gardens is just a 3-minute walk from København Hovedbanegård Station.

Nyhavn

Nyhavn, or New Harbor, is a beautiful spot that reeks of a long heritage filled with salty sailor stories and literary exploits. The colorful, picturesque buildings that line the canal here are the stars of innumerable Denmark postcards. Hans Christian Andersen lived here. You can take a hydrofoil to Sweden from here or simply stroll in this charming quarter and easily spend an hour or two here and visit the following places of interest in and around this historical area:

- **King's New Square** - This is the largest square in the city and was built by Christian V in 1670. There is an equestrian statue in honor of him.

- **Royal Danish Theater** - It is both a performing arts institution and a venue. This theater was founded in 1748 to serve the artistic needs of the then-Danish king. Today, it presents multi-genre concerts in addition to Royal Danish ballet and opera.

- **Memorial Anchor** - Situated at the base of the Nyhavn Canal, this maritime memorial was built in memory of the Danish sailors who died in WWII.

Thy National Park

Situated in Northwest Jutland, The Thy National Park is Denmark's biggest pocket of wilderness. The beaches in this place are washed by the North Sea Waves, while the high sand dunes offer a glorious sight. Dune heaths and gorgeous lakes are found behind the high sand dunes. Even further inland, you will find dark and impenetrable forests.

A significant portion of the country's dune area is found in the Thy National Park. The sparse vegetation here is influenced by dune conditions, including shifting sands, dune slopes and their orientation, lime content, and a considerable distance from groundwater tables.

Vegetation on dune heaths, on the other hand, is characterized by dwarf shrubs dominated by heather and crowberry. The biggest dune heaths in the Thy National Park are Alvande Klithede, Hanstholm Natural Reserve, and Vangsa Klithede. Red deer, adder, and otters inhabit these dune heaths.

There are over 200 lakes in the Thy National Park. Most of these lakes are lobelia lakes characterized by low levels of nutrients, sandy beds, and crystal-clear water. These lakes are home to underwater plants such as pillwort, quillwort, etc.

The Black Sun

The Black Sun is one of the most breathtaking natural phenomena found only in Denmark. The Danes call it the "Sort Sol." It can be seen in southwestern Jutland during two different periods, including from mid-March to mid-April and from August until October.

The best views of the Black Sun are on Ribe Island near the Wadden Sea and in the Todden marshlands. Sort Sol refers to the incredible formations of hundreds and thousands of starlings that migrate for their next breeding season at the turn of the season.

The "dance of the million birds," as it is called, happens around dusk when these birds rise up into the sky and move in unison. They make amazing turns in their flight and often appear to cover the setting sun completely. The spellbinding sight of the undulating blackness of the flying birds against the splendorous colors of the setting sun lasts for about 20-30 minutes. A sight that should not be missed while in Denmark.

Wadden Sea National Park

The Wadden Sea National Park is Denmark's largest national park and is located in an area that is a unique combination of mud and sand. This national park, therefore, has both saltwater and freshwater habitats. Many beaches and wetlands also form part of the demography of the Wadden Sea National Park.

This park is ideal for bird-watching because it is situated at the central point of the Eastern Atlantic migratory routes. The sea near the Esberg Harbor is home to spotted seals. The islands of Wadden Sea Rømø, Mandø, and Fanø, rife with dune heaths, forests, sea, and fauna, offer amazing holiday and tourist experiences for visitors.

The Ribe Viking Museum is located in the precincts of this national park. The Viking museum holds reconstructed Viking settlements and authentic artifacts. You can get a glimpse of how Vikings lived in the days of yore. Visitors can also participate in the daily activities.

Legoland Billund Resort

The land of the original Legos, Billund houses Legoland, is one of Denmark's most popular and unmissable tourist destinations. Lego lions greet you at the doorstep. You can step into large homes made of Lego. And, of course, white sandy beaches to discover will all be part of your Legoland tour.

The Legoland Billund Resort, located very close to the original Lego factory, opened its doors to visitors on 7th June 1968. It was originally built to promote the toy business started by Ole Kirk Christiansen. The design for Legoland is given to Dagny Holm, one of the cousins of the Christiansen family. Today, the park extends to 45 acres.

There are admission-free options such as playgrounds, town squares, and the Tree of Life, all made with Lego bricks. There are paid options if you want special experiences, and each experience has a different color code aligned with the Lego color code. Red stands for creativity, yellow for emotions, green for role-playing, and blue for cognitive challenges. Legoland is indisputably the largest tourist attraction in Denmark.

Øresund Bridge

This bridge connecting Denmark and Sweden took decades to plan and implement. This 12-km railway (and double track at that) and motorway bridge runs across the Øresund Strait between Denmark and Sweden. It runs from Copenhagen to the port of Malmo on the Sweden side. It is a stunning piece of engineering and is a must-visit tourist spot in Denmark. Here are some interesting, fun facts about the Øresund Bridge:

- The construction began in 1995 and became operational in 2000.

- It has the biggest concrete segments in the world.

- Tunnels were built instead of raising the bridge at many points to prevent interference with the air traffic of Copenhagen Airport.

- The heads of state from both Denmark and Sweden were present for the official opening ceremony.

- The bridge improved the economic and innovative outcomes on both sides.

Christiansborg Palace and Amalienborg Palace

The fortifications of Copenhagen City were built in the area of the Christiansborg Palace by Bishop Absalon in 1167 ACE. Located on the island of Slotsholmen, Copenhagen, today, the Christiansborg Palace is the seat of the Danish government. It is home to the Prime Minister's Office, the Parliament, and the Supreme Court and, therefore, can be called the "power base" of the Kingdom of Denmark.

The royal household still uses several parts of this palace, many of which are open to the public. The ruins of Bishop Absalon's castle (which was destroyed in the 14th century) and the medieval fort can be seen even today.

The Amalienborg Palace was built as a home for the nobility. There are four palaces forming an octagon facing a common central square. The royal household moved here when a fire broke out and destroyed the Christiansborg Palace in 1794. The blue-uniformed and bearskins-clad Soldiers of the Royal Guard are a special attraction for tourists visiting the Amalienborg Palace.

Our Savior's Church

This 17th-century church is easily one of the most famous landmarks in Copenhagen. A 400-step spiral serpentine staircase is a huge draw for tourists. Over 200,000 visitors climb these steps (the last 150 of them are outside) annually for a stunning view of Copenhagen from the top, where there is a statue of Our Savior on a globe.

The iconic bell tower of this church has six large bells and a 48-bell clarion which plays melodies daily that can be heard throughout the neighborhood. Access to the staircase can be had only with prior bookings.

National Museum of Denmark, Copenhagen

The National Museum (Nationalmuseet) is a walking distance from Tivoli Gardens and is replete with artifacts of Danish history and culture covering more than 14,000 years. The museum houses the famous 2,000-year-old bronze sun chariot, the Trundholm Sun Chariot, that was discovered in Denmark.

The Nationalmuseet also houses Viking artifacts, Egyptian mummies, Danish silver and porcelain, and Gothic and Romanesque church trimmings. Antique furniture and clothing from the 18th and 19th-century royal households also adorn this wonderful museum. The largest cultural museum of Denmark is located within the precincts of the Prince's Palace, which was built in 1743-44.

Kronborg Castle

This UNESCO heritage site is the setting of Shakespeare's Hamlet. Located in Helsingor (the most important transit point for Jewish safety evacuation during WWII), Kronborg Palace is a must-see, even for those who have only a passing interest in the life and works of the Bard-of-Avon. King Christian III built this castle as a fortress to protect Copenhagen from invaders. Some of the amazing things to see in this castle are (apart from its opulent walls):

- The stunning 16th-century Great Hall

- The statue and an exhibition about the Viking Chief Holger Dansk

- A maritime museum

Sometimes, actors placed all over the palace bring alive the characters from Hamlet. Interestingly, Kronborg was once used as a prison, and the convicts were made to work on the fortress's fortifications.

Viking Ship Museum

Located at a 40-minute car drive from Copenhagen on Route 21, the Viking Ship Museum or the Vikingeskibsmuseet gives visitors a chance to see how the highly skilled Viking navigators built and sailed their boats and ships. A boatyard right next to the museum uses conventional boat-building methods to recreate Viking ships.

The Viking Ship Hall, located at the center of the museum, holds five ships that were used during the Viking Age. These five ships were used to form a protective barrier on Roskilde Fjord. This museum was built in 1969 with the sole purpose of exhibiting the five newly excavated Skuldelev ships.

Den Gamle By

Den Gamle By in Aarhus is a living open-air history museum giving visitors an opportunity to experience three different times in the history of Denmark. There are three neighborhoods created in Den Gamle by representing the following periods in the country:

- The mid-19th century

- The 1020s

- 1974

Everything about these periods has been recreated in this museum, including the business, architecture, domestic lives and homes, roads, and people wearing costumes belonging to the respective period. In addition, Den Gamle By houses many individual museums, including the

Toy Museum, Danish Poster Museum, Gallery of Decorative Arts, and more.

Hans Christian Andersen Museum

Denmark and Hans Christian Andersen are almost synonymous. His stories and fairy tales have captured the imagination of not only his native country but the entire world. A visit to Denmark must include a visit to the museum dedicated to this outstanding writer. The Hans Christian Andersen Museum dates back to 1908 and is full of information and details regarding his life and works.

You can see an amazing array of artifacts and mementos from his life and his artworks and sketches too. His works are brought to life through podcasts. The scenes from his autobiography adorn the walls and ceilings of the domed hall.

Funen Village and The Faroe Islands

This open-air museum is also related to Hans Christian Andersen. This living history museum brings alive the Denmark of the 19th century by recreating the world of Hans Christian Andersen as he wrote his amazing fairy tales. Partially timbered farmhouses with thatched roofs make the experience of this village authentic.

You can interact with actors and interpreters and explore the farms, homes, and workshops to learn more about the writer's life and his writing inspirations. Farm animals and cooking demonstrations enhance the experience of this living history museum.

The Faroe Islands lie about 600 km west of the Norwegian coast and are part of the Kingdom of Denmark, although it has its own self-governing body. The Faroe Islands is an archipelago of 18 main islands and hundreds of smaller ones, all of which are characterized by beautiful meadows, steep rocky coasts, hills, fjords, and more.

The moderate temperature of the waters of these islands attracts a variety of marine life to this place. You can see a wide variety of seals, fish, and whales. It is a perfect getaway for birdwatchers and anglers.

Ten Interesting Facts about Denmark Tourism

1. Trains in Denmark give excellent offers to tourists. European citizens can buy the InterRail Denmark Pass, wherein they can take unlimited train journeys for 8 days a month. For global citizens, the Eurail Denmark Pass allows access to railway services in 33 European countries.

2. King Christian VIII gave a five-year charter to Georg Carstensen, the founder of Tivoli, because he thought that when people are having fun at an amusement park, then they will not worry about politics.

3. Today, Kronborg Castle is better known as Hamlet's Castle. Although we do not know if Shakespeare visited the Kronborg Castle, it is documented that many actors during his time visited it.

4. Another nine old Viking ships were excavated from the Roskilde Fjord in the 1990s during the expansion of the shipyard. These excavations are ongoing and not yet completed.

5. While Danish is taught in the Faroe Islands schools, Faroese is this self-governing territory's national language.

6. The James Bond movie "No Time to Die" was filmed in the Faroe Islands.

7. Over 50 million guests and tourists have visited Legoland since the day of its opening.

8. Hans Christian Andersen's childhood home, located to the southwest of

Odense Cathedral, is also part of the museum in Odense.

9. For safety reasons, the tower of Our Savior's Church remains closed and inaccessible to the public when there are heavy winds and/or rain/snow.

10. The Oresund Bridge was named after a Nordic television series called "The Bridge." The series was shot in and around the area of this bridge.

Danish Quiz to Test Yourself and Others

Questions

1. What are the two colors on the Dannebrog?

2. Name the current Danish monarch.

3. What is the capital of Denmark?

4. Which are the two self-governing independent territories that are part of Denmark?

5. Name the creator of Lego.

6. What is the population of the Faroe Islands?

7. Denmark has the world's oldest flag. (True/False)

8. Name the oldest amusement park in the world.

9. Tap water in Denmark is very unhygienic and cannot be drunk. (True/False)

10. Which Danish actor played Jamie Lannister in Game of Thrones?

11. Who is the famous Danish writer of fairy tales?

12. How many letters are there in the Danish language?

13. What is the Danish word for cozy togetherness?

14. The Danish pastry was invented in Denmark. (True / False)

15. If you are unmarried by your 25 birthday, what is showered on you?

16. If you remain unmarried on your 30th birthday, what is showered on you?

17. How many regions is Denmark divided into? When did this come into existence?

18. Which sport did Peter Schmeichel play?

19. Denmark was neutral during WWI. (True/False)

20. Which is the first brick cathedral in Denmark?

Answers:

1. Red and white

2. Queen Margrethe II

3. Copenhagen

4. The Faroe Islands and Greenland

5. Ole Kirk Christiansen

6. About 50,000

7. True

8. Bakken in Denmark

9. False

10. Nikolaj Coster-Waldau

11. Hans Christian Andersen

12. 29

13. Hygge

14. False; it was brought to Denmark by Austrian immigrants

15. Cinnamon

16. Pepper

17. Five regions came into existence in 2007

18. Football

19. True

20. Roskilde Cathedral

Conclusion

Denmark is a small yet big country not only in terms of size but also in terms of happy people. Happiness and hygge are deeply intertwined into the fabric of Danish society, and as a visitor, you will also be drawn into its warm, cozy hug.

Innumerable, beautiful islands nestling in blue-green waters make up this wondrous country. Denmark offers everything you desire: offbeat locales, popular tourist spots, excellent and economical public transport, delicious food, the exclusive Black Sun, and medieval towns and cities steeped in history and folklore.

The more you learn about this gorgeous nation, the more you will enjoy your trip to the country. Warm and friendly people welcome you and share their happiness secrets. Use this book to learn more about Denmark before you set out on a fun-filled holiday there.

Here's one last interesting tidbit about Denmark before concluding this book:

The Danish people love and respect democracy and show this love persistently at every election. The voter turnout in Denmark has been consistently high.

One last word from the author

Of all the books to choose from, thank you very much for choosing Danish Trivia Book and reading all the way to the end!

If you think this book has lived up to your expectations (or more), you are more than welcome to write that in a review. Likewise, if you thought the book contained only things you could have easily found on Google or YouTube, I'd love to know!

What to read next: If you enjoyed this book, check out my other Trivia books!

References

"10 BEST Places to Visit in Denmark - UPDATED 2023 (with Photos & Reviews)." Tripadvisor, www.tripadvisor.in/Attractions-g189512-Activities-Denmark.html.

"12 Ways You Can Get Happy in Denmark." VisitDenmark, www.visitdenmark.com/denmark/things-do/danish-culture/get-happy.

"18 Wild Animals in Denmark [Wildlife in Denmark]." Kevmrc.com, 19 Oct. 2022, www.kevmrc.com/animals-in-denmark.

77 Fun Facts about Denmark You Need to Know. 5 May 2021, wonderfulwanderings.com/denmark-facts/.

"Best Universities in Denmark 2022." Student, 20 Sept. 2021, www.timeshighereducation.com/student/best-universities/best-universities-denmark

Birbeck, Andrew. "17 Top-Rated Tourist Attractions in Denmark | PlanetWare." Planetware.com, 2019, www.planetware.com/tourist-attractions/denmark-dk.htm.

"Church of Our Savior | Church." VisitCopenhagen, www.visitcopenhagen.com/copenhagen/planning/church-our-saviour-gdk410659.

"Danish Immigration - Danish Museum." Museum of Danish America, www.danishmuseum.org/explore/danish-american-culture/immigration#.

"Denmark Country Profile - National Geographic Kids." Geography, 21 Mar. 2014, kids.nationalgeographic.com/geography/countries/article/denmark.

"Discover the Ships That Took Leif Erikson to North America." History Hit, www.historyhit.com/locations/the-viking-ship-museum/#.

"English | Find Information about Bakken in English." Www.bakken.dk, www.bakken.dk/english/.

"Fun Facts about Denmark." VisitDenmark, www.visitdenmark.com/denmark/things-do/danish-culture/fun-facts.

"Gefjun." Norse Mythology for Smart People, norse-mythology.org/gefjun/.

"Gorm the Old." Follow the Vikings, www.followthevikings.com/discover/famous-vikings/gorm-the-old.

History of Denmark. "History of Denmark." Denmark.dk, 2011, denmark.dk/people-and-culture/history.

"How to Get around Denmark with Public Transport." VisitDenmark, www.visitdenmark.com/denmark/plan-your-trip/public-transport.

https://www.facebook.com/swedishnomad. "25 Interesting Facts about Denmark - Swedish Nomad." Swedish Nomad, 4 Oct. 2018, www.swedishnomad.com/interesting-facts-about-denmark/.

"If You're Still Single at 25 in Denmark, People Throw Spices All over You in the Street - and It Only Gets Worse as You Get Older." Business Insider, www.businessinsider.in/strategy/if-youre-still-single-at-25-in-denmark-people-throw-spices-all-over-you-in-the-street-and-it-only-gets-worse-as-you-get-older/articleshow/62936377.cms.

International, The. "Royalty in the Land of Equality." The International, 2 July 2021, www.the-intl.com/post/royalty-in-the-land-of-equality.

McKay, Andrew. "15 Fun Facts about Denmark." Life in Norway, 25 June 2019, www.lifeinnorway.net/denmark-facts/.

National Museum of Denmark. "Christianity Comes to Denmark - National Museum of Denmark." National Museum of Denmark, 2019, en.natmus.dk/historical-knowledge/denmark/prehistoric-period-until-1050-ad/the-viking-age/religion-magic-death-and-rituals/christianity-comes-to-denmark/.

"Nature." Eng.nationalparkthy.dk, eng.nationalparkthy.dk/experience-the-national-park/nature/.

Nikel, David. "10 Fascinating Facts about the Faroe Islands." Life in Norway, 31 Mar. 2022, www.lifeinnorway.net/faroe-islands-facts/.

"Nyhavn (Copenhagen) - All You Need to Know before You Go." Tripadvisor, www.tripadvisor.in/Attraction_Review-g189541-d207265-Reviews-Nyhavn-Copenhagen_Zealand.html.

olaf. "Black Sun in Denmark : The Most Beautiful Spectacle You Can See." Visit Denmark.net, 23 Nov. 2012, denmark.net/black-sun-denmark/.

sarfraz.malik@prhacker.com. "Constitution Day — June 5." National Today, 5 June 2021, nationaltoday.com/constitution-day-denmark/.

"The 10 Largest Lakes in Denmark." WorldAtlas, 9 Apr. 2019, www.worldatlas.com/articles/the-10-largest-lakes-in-denmark.html.

"The History of Danish Neutrality Policy during World War 1." THE VELUX FOUNDATIONS, 4 Apr. 2018, veluxfoundations.dk/en/history-danish-neutrality-policy-during-world-war-1-food-waste-and-danish-welfare-state#.

The Many Trees of Denmark – SabinoCanyon.com. www.sabinocanyon.com/the-many-trees-of-denmark/.

"Top 10 Facts about LEGOLAND Billund Resort." Discover Walks Blog, 5 Sept. 2022, www.discoverwalks.com/blog/copenhagen/top-10-facts-about-legoland-billund-resort/.

"Top 10 Fascinating Facts about Kronborg Castle." Discover Walks Blog, 9 Sept. 2022, www.discoverwalks.com/blog/denmark/top-10-fascinating-facts-about-kronborg-castle/

"Top 10 Interesting Facts about Øresund Bridge." Discover Walks Blog, 17 Oct. 2022, www.discoverwalks.com/blog/denmark/top-10-interesting-facts-about-oresund-bridge/.

"Top 10 Intriguing Facts about National Museum of Denmark." Discover Walks Blog, 9 Sept. 2022, www.discoverwalks.com/blog/denmark/top-10-intriguing-facts-about-national-museum-of-denmark/.

"Top 20 Most Common Plants in Denmark." PictureThis, www.picturethisai.com/region/Denmark.html.

"Why Are Danes Celebrating the Fourth of July?" Christian Science Monitor, www.csmonitor.com/USA/2014/0704/Why-are-Danes-celebrating-the-Fourth-of-July.

© Copyright 2023 - All rights reserved.

The content contained within this book may not be reproduced, duplicated, or transmitted without direct written permission from the author or the publisher.

Under no circumstances will any blame or legal responsibility be held against the publisher, or author, for any damages, reparation, or monetary loss due to the information contained within this book, either directly or indirectly.

Legal Notice:

This book is copyright protected. It is only for personal use. You cannot amend, distribute, sell, use, quote or paraphrase any part, or the content within this book, without the consent of the author or publisher.

Disclaimer Notice:

Please note the information contained within this document is for educational and entertainment purposes only. All effort has been executed to present accurate, up to date, reliable, complete information. No warranties of any kind are declared or implied. Readers acknowledge that the author is not engaging in the rendering of legal, financial, medical, or professional advice. The content within this book has been derived from various sources. Please consult a licensed professional before attempting any techniques outlined in this book.

By reading this document, the reader agrees that under no circumstances is the author responsible for any losses, direct or indirect, that are incurred as a result of the use of information contained within this document, including, but not limited to, errors, omissions, or inaccuracies.

www.ingramcontent.com/pod-product-compliance
Lightning Source LLC
LaVergne TN
LVHW041432170726
843492LV00008B/2577